The Go

CW00377079

Bugs, gotchas and guidelines for go programmers

CIPHER PRESS

CONTENTS

Introduction

About Go

The Go language spec is deceptively simple to read, with only 25 keywords and few data structures.

The syntax is very like other languages in the C family, and programmers coming from other languages with this heritage will find it easy to get started with the language, however it can be difficult to assimilate the culture of radical minimalism. Some programmers feel keenly the lack of familiar tools which Go simply leaves out - inheritance, assertions, exceptions, the ternary operator, enums, and generics are all missing by design. In addition, the strict rules on formatting and the culture of limited dependencies and minimal abstraction can feel restrictive, but these very deliberate omissions also provide some concrete advantages. The corollary to this culture of simplicity, and one of the most rewarding aspects of programming in Go, is the accessibility and simplicity of the standard library code and many of the libraries available - Go code is easy to read as well as write.

Also invaluable is the clarity and stability of the standard library, encapsulated in the Go 1 promise made way back in 2012 (which still holds today), or Brad Fitzpatrick's whimsical description of the language as asymptotically approaching boring. If you build an app today, it will compile with minimal or no changes until Go 2. While being difficult for the maintainers, this is a liberating promise for Go programmers as it makes this level of the ecosystem very stable.

If you're looking for a cutting-edge language which explores recent research, or one which favours terse abstractions, Go is not for you – Go is boring by design.

Bugs in Go programs

Programs in Go, like those in any other language, are subject to bugs.

Some are caused by unexpected data - a look at the Trophy Cabinet of bugs found by Go Fuzz should disabuse us of the notion that most bugs are esoteric or difficult to defend against, or even specific to Go as a language. Often the same errors crop up again and again – bounds not checked or nil pointers. The most common bugs encountered (even by experienced programmers) are:

- Index out of range
- Slice bounds out of range
- Nil pointer dereferences

These are trivial errors, but are easy to make in any sufficiently large program, and are usually due to expectations about data passed in from outside the program which don't hold true (hence they are easier to find with a fuzzer).

There are also a few mistakes which are easy to make when learning Go which a fuzzer might not detect, such as not correctly passing values to a goroutine within a range loop, misuse of an API, or lack of familiarity with the tradeoffs in the design of slices or strings in Go. These are the classes of bugs which this book will hopefully help the reader avoid.

Why read this book?

Typically Go programmers get up to speed quickly and feel productive within days or weeks, but it can be harder to assimilate the culture and be aware of the subtle problems that can occur. *The Go Bestiary* provides a quick guide to allow a programmer who has some experience in other languages get started quickly in Go, while being aware of the idioms to use and areas where there might be bugs lurking in their new Go code. The book presents a mix of advice for structuring your Go programs and descriptions of common mistakes to avoid, with liberal code examples, to help ease you into using Go.

If you're familiar with Go but not an expert, hopefully there will also be a few interesting facts about the language you haven't yet uncovered, and some potential bugs which you might not be aware of. You may want to skip the sections on setup and packages in this case, as they will cover familiar ground.

If you're new to Go, but experienced in other languages, you'll find succinct descriptions of the most important differences in Go which usually trip up learners (for example declaring strings, strings vs runes, copying slices, using goroutines within a for loop), descriptions of bugs which beginners often fall prey to, and plenty of detail about unique aspects of the language like goroutines and slices.

Setting up Go

If you have already written and compiled Go code before you can probably skip this section.

To get up and running with Go, you should follow the Getting Started instructions on the go website. If you're on Mac or Windows there is an installer which will make life easier for you and is the recommended route to installation – you can find the latest installers at the download page.

You can use homebrew to install go on macs, but you're probably better sticking with the official installer package available on golang.org. Do not use both.

Setting GOPATH

GOPATH is the bugbear of many new users of Go, but it is simply a place to store go code and binaries. This environment variable was introduced in order to make it simple for the Go tool to install dependencies automatically, and to keep all go code in one place. Since Go 1.7 this has defaulted to:

```
$HOME/go
```

GOPATH contains three directories:

- bin - for installed binaries
- src - for go source code
- pkg - a cache for intermediate build products

You may want to add your `$GOPATH/bin` folder to your path so that installed go tools are found automatically.

So you don't need to set it explicitly, but you do need to put all your go code under `$GOPATH/src` for go tools to work correctly. This is where code will be installed when you run go get, and this is where your dependencies will be stored. There is no concept of versioning in the go get tool, so it will fetch the latest master of any dependencies.

While it can be frustrating for newcomers, you should accept that all go code will live in your `GOPATH` — there are workarounds to attempt to keep code elsewhere, but the standard tools at present assume you use `GOPATH` for your code. You may find projects sometimes use folders called pkg or src internally inside their main go gettable folder, but this is unrelated to `GOPATH` and is just a way of organising their code. The only special src folder is that at the root of your `GOPATH`.

The similarly named ENV variable `GOROOT` need only be set **if installing to a custom location**. In most circumstances you can ignore `GOROOT`, as it is not required for a normal Go setup.

Checking your setup

To test your setup and confirm go is installed correctly, try the go command:

```
go version
```

You should see output something like this telling you the go version and the installed platform of the go tools:

go version go1.9 darwin/amd64

Then try a very simple program to check that your go setup is working. First save the following text file in `$GOPATH/src/hello.go` with UTF-8 encoding:

```go
// Package main contains the entrypoint of the program
package main

// The imports list dependencies
import (
    "fmt"
)

// The function main is the entry point of your program
func main() {

    // Print a string to stdout
    fmt.Printf("hello, 世界\n")

}
```

and use the go command to run it:

```
go run $GOPATH/src/hello.go
```

You should see the output:

hello, 世界

If you don't, your installation is not working and you should recheck the steps above and check the Installation instructions on the Go website.

Cross Compiling

You can use Go to compile programs not just for the platform you're on, but for another supported platform, like Windows or Linux if you're working on a mac. This makes it very easy to deploy programs as single binaries, without worrying about the dependencies or building on your server. For example if you want to build the hello.go program above for the Linux platform, you could use:

```
GOOS=linux GOARCH=arm go build -o hello-linux $GOPATH/src
/hello.go
```

This will give you a binary which runs on linux arm (or any other platform you choose), without any extra fuss.

Editors

Some of the most widely used editors for Go programmers, roughly in order of popularity are: VSCode, Vim (with vim-go), IntelliJ IDEA, Emacs, and Atom. Since go just requires text files and doesn't require any special support, you can easily switch between editors, but make sure your editor has support for running go fmt on save, and ideally support for looking up definitions from within the editor. Another useful tool for browsing go source code is sourcegraph (which happens to be written in Go).

You should always run go fmt on your code, and ideally a linter like gometalinter too. Try to set up your editor initially you run these on save. Almost all public go code is run through go fmt, and if interacting with other go programmers, this is taken as a given. Most editors have a go plugin like vscode-go or vim-go which will take care of this for you.

Linter Warnings

If you pay attention to linter warnings, and make sure you fix them all, you'll find your go code is more idiomatic and you should avoid common errors like executing goroutines with values from a range loop.

Dependencies

> Duplication is far cheaper than the wrong abstraction
> Sandi Metz

There is a culture of limiting dependencies in Go, unlike some other ecosystems, the design of Go does not encourage importing libraries for trivial functions. If you're coming from node this will come as a shock, but you should try to adapt to the very different culture, as there are some advantages.

The biggest problem with dependencies in the long term is entropy over time - the more dependencies you have, the greater the chance of changes which break your build (for security, or api changes, or new features), and the more painful it becomes to keep up to date with the ecosystem you've bought into. This is why it is useful to limit your dependencies, and explicitly version those you have, and why vendoring (taking a copy of dependencies frozen at a given version) has become an accepted solution in the Go community to importing dependencies.

Although Go is statically typed which offers some protection, you should not assume that if dependencies change and your code compiles everything is working. A change to a dependency might make subtle changes to defaults or values which while they still compile result in the unexpected behaviour. The only solution to managing dependencies is to freeze them at the import version and inspect changes carefully before upgrading.

Resources

You should start by working through the Go Tour, you should then skim Effective Go (you will want to come back to this later). You should read the docs from the standard library, which contain lots of examples, and finally you might want to refer to Go By Example - a set of code snippets.

Go Playground

The Go Playground is a web service that runs on golang.org's servers. The service receives a Go program, compiles, links, and runs the program inside a sandbox, then returns the output. The intention is for go playground links to last forever (in internet time that's at least a few years).

The playground has certain limitations, mostly for security reasons it restricts certain operations like writing files or accessing the network, and the time is the same for each run. There are also limits on execution time and on CPU and memory usage. See Inside the Go playground for more details.

Stack Overflow

You can find the answer to many questions about Go on stackoverflow, in particular small questions of grammar. A few tips for using this resource:

- Be sure to search for related questions with the go tag before you post your own.
- Try to post a link to a reproduction of the problem on play.golang.org
- Include the full code and an explanation of the problem
- Accepted answers on stack overflow are sometimes wrong

Community

There are many partially overlapping online communities for Go which vary greatly in style and content.

The Go Forum is a friendly place to ask beginner questions

The Go Time podcast interviews luminaries in the Go community and beyond with a focus on Go

Golang News provides links to articles, videos etc. about Go

The Go subreddit is another source of links and news

Women Who Go organises meetups for women and gender minorities who use Go all over the world

The Gopher Slack has an active community of slackers

The Golang Nuts mailing list has a lot of activity if you prefer mailing lists

There are many videos from Go conferences at GopherVids

Just for func is a great podcast on Go programming by the inimitable @francesc

There are a huge number of meetups and conferences about Go, you can find more on the Community page of the wiki.

Writing Idiomatic Go

For a guide to idiomatic Go, you can refer to the wiki Code Review Comments, which is a summary of comments made on contributions to the Go project and a lot of good advice on structure and names in Go code.

Go is opinionated about formatting (as about so much else) and provides the tool go fmt to enforce the suggested formatting. There is one standard style for code, including brace positions, spacing etc, enforced by the tools. This has been embraced by users of go, and it turns out it doesn't really matter where you place your braces or whether you use spaces or tabs, so you can now spend your time worrying about more important things, like whether go should have generics.

Strings

Source code in Go is in the UTF-8 encoding. This means string literals you create will be UTF strings, and the source files themselves are UTF-8. The string type offers no such guarantees, it stores an array of bytes, but by convention it is usually UTF-8, and you should convert to Unicode at the boundaries of your app. For a detailed overview of the internal workings of strings in Go see Strings, bytes, runes and characters in Go on the official Go blog.

Declaring strings

Quotation marks in Go source code behave slightly differently from other languages.

If you use double quotes you will get a string, and can include escape codes, like \n for newline:

```
// hello is a string containing newline & tab
hello := "hello\n\tworld"
```

```
hello
world
```

If you use back quotes escape codes will not be interpreted, and the string can contain raw newlines:

```
// hello is a string with no newline
hello := `hello world\n`
```

This results in no newline:

> hello world\n

If you use single quotes, you won't create a string at all, these create a rune:

```
hello := 'h' // a rune
```

> h

This is why if you try to define a string with single quotes, you'll get an error:

```
// This is not a valid string
hello := 'hello'
```

> 'invalid character literal (more than one character)'

Multi-line strings

To define multi-line strings, including literal control characters like newline, use back quotes, for example:

```
// A string containing a newline after hello
`hello
  world`
```

Runes

Runes in Go represent a code point in unicode, rather than a character. They may be a single character, or they may be part of a character or a modifier. They are an alias for the type `int32` .

For example the string:

Hello, 世界

Is represented by these bytes:

> [72 101 108 108 111 44 32 228 184 150 231 149 140]

but is represented by these runes:

> [72 101 108 108 111 44 32 19990 30028]

as you can see if you range over it (see below).

Range on Strings

If you range on a string, you will receive the runes which make up the string, not the bytes. In an ASCII string every byte corresponds exactly to one rune, so ranging "hello" will return:

> 'h', 'e', 'l', 'l', 'o'

and ranging over "日本語" will return the runes, not the bytes:

> '日', '本', '語'

Index on Strings

Somewhat confusingly, given how ranging works, if you take the index of a string you'll get the byte at that index, not the rune:

```
s := "日本語"
// This returns a byte at index 2
b := s[2]
fmt.Println(b)
```

Returns the third byte, not the third rune as you might expect:

```
165
```

Trimming strings

The strings package contains many useful functions for manipulating text, and each one is documented. Some might not do exactly what you expect from the name, for example strings.Trim does not trim a given suffix or prefix:

```
s := "les mots, et les choses"
t := strings.Trim(s,"les ")
fmt.Println(t)
```

The result may be unexpected:

```
mots, et les cho
```

This function takes a **cutset** string – a list of characters to trim. If you want to trim a full prefix or suffix, use strings.TrimPrefix or strings.TrimSuffix:

```
s := "les mots, et les choses"
t := strings.TrimPrefix(s,"les ")
fmt.Println(t)
```

Which will remove the suffix or prefix provided as you would expect.

Formatting Strings

The usual Printf and Sprintf variants are available in the fmt package, so that you can format strings using a template string and variables. The formats accepted are detailed in the strings package documentation. %v prints the value in a default format and is useful for debugging.

```
fmt.Printf("%s at %v", "hello world", time.Now())
// Print to a string
s := fmt.Sprintf("%s at %v", "hello world", time.Now())
```

Encodings

Most of the time when working with unicode strings in Go you won't have to do anything special. If you need to convert from another encoding like Windows 1252 you can use the encoding package under golang.org/x/text. There are also some other utility packages for dealing with text there. The golang.org/x libraries are slightly less stable than the go standard library and are not part of the official distribution, but have many useful utilities.

Translating encodings

The go external package text/encoding packages provide utilties for translating strings from Go's native UTF-8 to popular encodings and back (such as UTF-16, EUC-JP, GBK and Big5). Encoders and Decoders are available for working with arrays of bytes or strings.

```
// Convert from Go's native UTF-8 to UTF-16
// using golang.org/x/text/encoding/unicode
s := "エヌガミ"

// Encode native UTF-8 to UTF-16
encoder := unicode.UTF16(unicode.LittleEndian, unicode.Us
eBOM).NewEncoder()
utf16, err := encoder.String(s)
if err != nil {
    fmt.Println(err)
}
fmt.Println("utf16:", utf16)
```

Strings are immutable

Strings in Go are immutable, you are not allowed to change
the backing bytes, and manipulating bytes directly can be
dangerous as the string *may* contain several bytes for each
character/rune.

Don't use pointers to strings

A string value is a fixed size and should not be passed as a
pointer.

Strings are never nil

You cannot assign nil to a string or compare nil to a string,
they have a zero value of "" and can never be nil, only the
zero value.

Converting Strings to Ints

You can use the strconv package to convert Strings to other types like ints and floats and back again.

```
// Itoa converts an int to a string
s := strconv.Itoa(99)
// Atoi converts a string to an int
i,_ := strconv.Atoi(s)
// Print both types
fmt.Printf("string:%s int:%d", s, i)
```

Returns

```
string:99 int:99
```

Parsing floats

Floats are imprecise and rounding can be unpredictable. When parsing them from strings and working with them, you need to be aware of this.

```
price := "655.18"
f, _ := strconv.ParseFloat(price, 64)
c := int(f * 100)
fmt.Printf("string:%s float:%f cents:%d", price, f, c)
```

```
string:655.18 float:655.180000 cents:65517
```

If parsing a float for a currency value, consider converting the string to a value in cents first, as you will have work to do anyway to strip currency amounts and deal with missing cents. You can then parse as an integer and avoid any problems with storing it as a float.

21

Reading text files

The easiest way to read an entire file is with ioutil, but unless the file is small (e.g. a config file) this can use a large amount of memory:

```go
b, err := ioutil.ReadFile("path/to/file")
if err != nil {
    fmt.Println("error reading file: %s", err)
}


fmt.Printf("%s", b)
```

So consider reading large files in chunks. You can read a line-based file with bufio.Scanner and the Scan function:

```go
file, err := os.Open("path/to/file")
if err != nil {
    fmt.Println("error opening file: %s", err)
    return
}
defer file.Close()
scanner := bufio.NewScanner(file)
for scanner.Scan() {
    fmt.Println("line:%s", scanner.Text())
}
if err := scanner.Err(); err != nil {
    fmt.Println("error reading file: %s", err)
}
```

Also consider that files conform to io.Reader and io.Writer from the io package, and can be used directly with functions which accept an io.Reader.

Structs & Types

A struct in Go is a sequence of fields, each of which has a name and type public and private rules are the same as names in packages - lowercase names are private, names starting with Uppercase are exported. Structs can also have methods, which allows them to fulfil interfaces. Structs do not inherit from each other, but they can embed another struct to gain its fields and behaviour. The embedder does not know anything about the struct it is embedded in and cannot access it.

Forget inheritance

During a Java user group meeting James Gosling (Java's inventor) was asked "If you could do Java over again, what would you change?". He replied: "I'd leave out classes"

Go eschews inheritance in favour of composition. If you're accustomed to building large hierarchies of types as a way of organising your data, you might find this jarring at first. Go interfaces provide polymorphism, so if your function needs something which Barks, it simply asks for a Barker. Go embedding provides composition, so if your Barker needs to Yap as well, it can embed a struct to do so. Go provides tools which solve the same problems as inheritance, without most of the downsides. You may find you need it less than you think.

Many developers coming to go from more complex OOP languages start by trying to reintroduce inheritance by using embedding. This will lead to frustration, because embedding does not work in the same way as inheritance, by design.

Composition is not inheritance

Composition can do some of the same things as inheritance, but it is not the same. For example, don't try to do this:

```go
package main

import (
    "fmt"
)

// Type A knows only about A, it cannot call B methods
type A struct{}

func (a A) Foo() { a.Bar() }
func (a A) Bar() { fmt.Println("This is a method on A") }

// Type B knows about A and B
type B struct{
  A // Embeds A - note this is not inhertance
}

// Type B attempts to redefine Bar()
// but type A doesn't know about it
func (b B) Bar() { fmt.Println("This is a method on B") }

func main() {
    B{}.Foo()
}
```

A.Foo will call A.Bar, not B.Foo as it might if B inherited from A, because A does not know about B.

Inheritance was deliberately left out of Go, so don't try to recreate it with composition. If you find yourself frustrated that embedded structs don't know about the embedder, you're not really composing functionality. Always try to use the simplest solution first (separate structs), and only use composition if you definitely need to share the same behaviour between two types.

Don't use this or self

While it is common in other languages, it is frowned upon in Go to use self or this in receiver names, instead use the first letter of the receiver. Go has no language support for these words, it does not use them as keywords as other languages do and it is therefore confusing to use them in a Go context.

Type assertions

Use a type assertion to check the type wrapped in an interface is of the expected type, or to retrieve the value, rather than attempting to use it without checks. If type assertions are used *without* the comma ok form, a panic ensues if the type is not as expected, so it's always better to use the comma ok form and check the boolean returned.

```
// Convert from interface back to underlying type int
var x interface{} = 7
a := x.(int)
fmt.Println("a is int:", a)


// Attempt to convert from interface to int with a string
var y interface{} = "hello"

// Check before use, no panic
b, ok := y.(int)
if !ok {
    fmt.Println("b is not int:", b)
}

// panic, because y is not of type int
//b = y.(int)
```

Nil pointer dereference

This error is usually caused by failing to check errors properly (i.e. using a value without checking that there were no errors), or storing a nil pointer and later trying to use it. **Check and handle all errors**. Never use _ as a shortcut in production code:

```
// Don't do this, value may well be invalid
value, _ := f()
...
```

Instead, always check errors:

```
// Do this
value, err := f()
if err != nil {
    // Deal with error
    return fmt.Errorf("msg %s",err)
}
// use value
...
```

Pointers vs Values for Methods

You can define methods either on the struct value or struct pointer. If unsure, you can follow these guidelines for deciding which to use:

- **If in doubt, use a pointer receiver**
- If the method modifies the receiver, it must be on a pointer receiver
- If the receiver is large, e.g. a big struct, it is cheaper to use a pointer receiver
- If the type is stored in a map or interface, it is not addressable and T cannot use *T methods
- If you need any pointer receivers, make them all pointer receivers

The outcome of these guidelines is that usually it's best to work with pointers to structs and thus to define methods on the pointer, not on the value. For small structs you may want to use values for efficiency, but for large structs or structs which modify themselves, you will want to use pointer receivers. There is more detail on the rules for pointer receivers at the end of this chapter in the section on Method Sets.

Pointers vs Values in Slices

As you'll probably want to use pointers to structs elsewhere in your code, it makes sense to use slices of pointers, rather than slices of values. This also lets you update the structs in the slice directly.

Pointers vs Values for constructors

When writing constructors, default to pointers to structs for the same reasons as above. You can certainly return plain structs or values, particularly for simple values, but typically simple values won't require a constructor.

Why do new and make exist?

You can probably get away without using `new` at all - it simple allocates a new instance of a type, and you can use &T{} instead.

`make` is required for used with maps, slices and channels to initialise them with a given size, for example:

```
// Using make with maps and slices
make(map[int]int)    // A map with no entries
make(map[int]int,10) // A map with 10 zero entries
make([]int, 10, 100) // A slice with 10 zero entries, and
 a capacity of 100
c := make(chan int)  // An unbuffered channel of integers
```

Enums

There are no enums in Go. Use the keyword iota to increment constants from a known base, so the closest to an enum is a set of constants in a file:

```go
// Describe the constants here
const (
    RoleAnon = iota
    RoleReader
    RoleAdmin
)
```

For more sophisticated control impose limits or provide string values by using a type:

```go
type Role struct {
  value int
}

func (e Role)SetValue(v int) {
  if v == RoleAnon || v = RoleReader || v = RoleAdmin {
    e.value = v
  }
}

func (e Role)Value(v int) {
    return e.value
}
```

Method Sets

You *normally* don't have to worry about method sets as the compiler will transform pointers or values to the other in order to use methods defined on the other as a convenience, but this breaks down in some circumstances. The exceptions to this are if a type is stored in a map, or stored in an Interface, or if you want to mutate the value of the receiver within the method. This is a gnarly detail, and effective go is somewhat confusing on this score:

> The rule about pointers vs. values for receivers is that value methods can be invoked on pointers and values, but pointer methods can only be invoked on pointers.

It should probably end with can only be invoked on pointers or addressable values. If you attempt to test this, you'll find that you **can** call pointer methods on struct values in most circumstances:

```go
type T struct{}

func (t T) Foo() { fmt.Println("foo") }
func (t *T) Bar() { fmt.Println("bar") }


func main() {
    // t can call methods Foo and Bar
    // as is is addressable
    // but beware if Bar() changes
    // the receiver changes will be lost
    t := T{}
    t.Foo()
    t.Bar() // compiler converts to (&t).Bar()

    // tp can call methods Foo and Bar
    tp := &T{}
    t.Foo()
    tp.Bar()
}
```

The compiler will try to help you by inserting dereferences for pointers or pointers for types where you try to call a method, but this won't work in all instances, it breaks down if your type is stored in a map, or stored in an interface:

```go
func main() {

    // You can call the pointer method on a pointer entry
 in a map
    mp := make(map[int]*T)
    mp[1] = tp
    mp[1].Foo() // Allowed
    mp[1].Bar() // Allowed

    // You cannot call the pointer method on a value entr
 y in a map
    m := make(map[int]T)
    m[1] = t
    m[1].Foo() // Allowed
    //m[1].Bar() // Not Allowed - cannot take the address
 of m[1]

    callFoo(tp) // Allowed
    callFoo(t)  // Allowed

    callBar(tp) // Allowed
    //callBar(t) // Not Allowed - Bar method has pointer
 receiver

}

func callBar(i I)  { i.Bar() }
func callFoo(i FI) { i.Foo() }
```

You can read more about this on this wiki entry on Method Sets.

Slices

Slices are views into arrays of data, offering an efficient way of working with arrays. They can share the same data, and simply store an offset into it. This is useful if you don't need to mutate the data but can lead to some subtle bugs if you assume every slice is independent. To get to grips with how slices work internally in Go, see Go Slices: usage and internals, and for an interesting overview of the reasons slices came to their current form, see Slices by Rob Pike on the Go blog.

Nil slices

The zero value of a slice is a nil slice. It has no underlying array, and has 0 length. It can be used without initialisation (unlike maps).

Slicing shares data

When you use the slice operator, be aware that the backing data will be shared, using the same underlying array. If you need an independent copy of a slice to manipulate the underlying data, take a copy of it first. After you slice, the new slice will be a view onto the same data, but further operations (like append) on that new slice may mean it is copied, so it is usually better not to rely on slices sharing data if you wish to mutate that data. This sharing of a backing store can be very useful if you don't need to change data but just use parts of it as it avoids extra allocations.

```
a := []int{0,1,2,3,4,5}
s := a[:]
s2 := s[1:3]
```

This can be confusing though if you don't recognise what is happening. For example if you take two slices of data, then append to one of them, the results for the other view into that data are unpredictable and depend on the length of data:

```
// start with an array
data := []int{0, 1, 2}

// Get two views on data, showing positions 0 and 1
a := data[0:1] // 0
b := data[1:2] // 1

a = append(a, 3, 4) // append two numbers to a, which
overwrites b
//    a = append(a, 3, 4, 5) // append three numbers
to a, growing the slice, leaving b alone

// the new slice a is as expected
println(a[0])
// but the values in b may surprise
println(b[0])
```

For this reason if mutating a slice with append, you may need to take a copy of data before using it elsewhere or face unexpected side effects. This bug may hit you if you use bytes.Split or similar functions to return sections of data from a slice of bytes.

Slicing retains the original

Slicing a slice doesn't copy the underlying array, so the full array will be kept in memory until it is no longer referenced. If you're just using a small part of a large slice, consider copying that new slice into another shorter one so that the original data can be released.

```go
// readHeader reads the file header
func readHeader(file string) {

    // Read data at file path
    b, _ := ioutil.ReadFile(file)

    // slice the data to truncate
    s := b[:12]

    // Copy the data we want to a new shorter slice
    c := make([]byte, len(s))
    copy(c, s)

    return c
}
```

Slicing is limited by cap

Conversely to indexes (from 0 to len), slicing is limited by cap, not by len, as stated in the spec, which may seem a little counter-intuitive, and you probably shouldn't rely on. This means in some circumstances you can retrieve the backing data for a slice even outside its range, as long as it is between len and cap. If you need to see the original data it is better to keep a copy of the original slice to make the intent clear.

Index out of range

One of the most common slice mistakes is to attempt to access an index past the length of an array or slice, due to programmer error. This will result in a panic at runtime:

> panic: runtime error: index out of range

While this may seem like a trivial mistake to make, it causes a panic at runtime, and you should take care to avoid it by always bounding index operations at the length of the slice. To catch this kind of error with varied input you should try running your code through go-fuzz. You can read more about how to use Go Fuzz in Fuzzing a DNS Parser.

Copying slices

To copy a slice and duplicate the backing data, use the built-in copy function. The destination comes first in the arguments to copy. Beware when copying - the minimum of len(dst) and len(src) is chosen as the length of the new slice, so the destination will need enough space to fit src. Do not attempt to copy into an empty slice as it will not expand automatically.

```go
// Make a new slice to copy
src := []int{1,2,3}
// Make sure dst has enough capacity for src
dst := make([]int, len(src))
// Copy from src to dst, n is the no of elements copied
n := copy(dst, src)
```

If you try to copy a src of length 100 into a destination slice of length 1, only 1 entry will be copied into the destination.

Appending elements

Use the built in append function to add an element to a slice.

```
var s []string
s = append(s,"hello")
fmt.Println(s)
```

Appending *may* create a new backing array, it's best not to rely on the slice argument not changing - the argument may change in length, and the slice returned may not be the slice which goes in. It does not create a copy of the slice and return it for every append, as this would waste a lot of memory. When you definitely need a copy (for example you need to preserve the original slice as well as mutate it), take a copy of the slice (or the part of the slice you need) first:

```
// Make a new slice
c := make([]byte, len(s))

// Take a copy
copy(c, s)
```

Because of this behaviour it is best to always assign the result of append to the same slice.

Appending slices

You can use the append function to concatenate slices, in combination with the variadic operator to turn the second slice argument into an array of elements.

```
s = append(s,b...)
```

Sorting

To sort a slice you can use sort.Slice from the sort package.
This package contains other helpers for operations such as
stable sorts, binary search, and reversing slices.

```
people := []struct {
        Name string
        Age  int
    }{
        {"Gopher", 7},
        {"Alice", 55},
        {"Vera", 24},
    }
sort.Slice(people, func(i, j int) bool {
  return people[i].Name < people[j].Name
})
```

Map on slices

Slices have been kept intentionally simple, which means
you'll be using the for range idiom a lot to perform operations
on them. There is no map or forEach function, just use a
range on the slice.

```
for _, v := range s {
    f(v)
}
```

Converting slice types

If you have a slice of []T and wish to convert it to a slice of type []interface{}, or vice versa, you will have to do it by hand with a for loop. They do not have the same representation in memory and there is no convenient way to do it.

```
t := []int{1, 2, 3, 4}
s := make([]interface{}, len(t))
for i, v := range t {
    s[i] = v
}
```

Passing slices to functions

Be aware when passing a slice to a function that while the slice itself is passed by value, it points to a backing array which does not change, even if the slice is copied, so modifying the elements of the slice passed in will modify elements of the original backing array.

Multi-dimensional slices

Go doesn't have multi-dimensional slices or maps, you have to create them by hand, initialising each subslice.

Maps

Maps in Go are hash tables, which provide fast access to values for a given key, one value per key. You can read more about maps in go in the Go maps in action article on the go blog.

Maps and Goroutines

Go maps are not thread safe. If you need to access a map across goroutines (for example in a handler), you should use a mutex to protect access and make it a private variable protected by that mutex. Any access to the map should lock the mutex first, perform the operation, and then unlock it again. You can also use a RWMutex if you have a lot of reads and few writes.

```go
type Data struct {
    // mu protects access to values
    mu sync.Mutex
    // values stores our data
    values map[int]int
}

func (d *Data)Add(k,v int) {
  d.mu.Lock()
  d.values[k] = v
  d.mu.Unlock()
}
```

Be careful when using mutexes or maps not to inadvertently make copies of them (for example if you passed Data below by value to a function, the mutex would be copied along with the data). For this reason you will sometimes see mutexes declared as pointers, but the important point is not to copy them (or their data).

It is often clearer to put the mutex right next to the data they protect; convention is to name them mu and place them above the field which they protect. You should very rarely need to explicitly initialise a mutex or use a pointer to a mutex, the zero value can be used directly as above.

Map values

You cannot take the address of map keys or values. You cannot assign to struct fields for structs stored as values in the map, they are immutable. You should instead store pointers in the map, and you can then mutate the structs those pointers refer to.

```
// Define a type
type T struct {F int}

// Define a map
m := map[int]T{1:{F:1}}

// Accessing fields on T is not allowed
m[1].F = 4
```

This produces the result:

cannot assign to struct field m[1].F in map

Key order

Maps have no defined order, and keys and values returned are randomised to enforce this.

```go
// Define a map
m := map[int]int{1: 1, 2: 2, 3: 3, 4: 4, 5: 5}
// Range 5 times
for i := 0; i < 5; i++ {
    // The order of keys and values is undefined
    for k, v := range m {
        fmt.Printf("(%d:%d)", k, v)
    }
    fmt.Println("")
}
```

The output of ranging on a map is not deterministic:

```
(2:2)(3:3)(4:4)(5:5)(1:1)
```

```
(1:1)(2:2)(3:3)(4:4)(5:5)
```

To range map keys in order, get the keys, sort them to some predefined order, then range the keys and get the values.

Keys not in the map

A map retrieval yields a zero value when the key is not present, so always check a key is present before using it if this distinction is important to you (for example if you want to treat an empty string stored in the map differently from a missing value).

```
key := "foo"

// You can check whether a value exists in the map
v, ok := m[key]
if ok {
  // do something with v
}

// Or you can simply get the value (a zero value if not p
resent)
v := m[key]
```

Nil Maps

Maps must always be initialised before use, the zero value is not useful.

```
// Allowed
var s []int
s = append(s,1)

// You must init a map before use
m := make(map[string]int, 10)

// This is ok
m["key"] = 1

// If you assign to a nil map - panic
var mnil map[string]int
mnil["key"] = 1
```

If you assign to a nil map panic ensues

panic: assignment to entry in nil map

A nil map behaves like an empty map when reading, so if you are sure you should only read from it, it is safe to use.

Use the right data structure

If you need fast random access, use a map (for example if storing cache items by key). If you need fast iteration or sorting, use a slice – iterating a map is significantly slower than iterating over a slice.

Goroutines

Prefix a function or method call with the `go` keyword to run the call in a new goroutine, asynchronously. The `go` keyword is one of the distinguishing features of Go, but it can lead to subtle bugs if not used carefully.

> Do not communicate by sharing memory; instead, share memory by communicating. – Rob Pike

Asynchronous execution

The simplest usage of a goroutine is simply to execute a function without waiting for a response. For example in a web handler to send a mail, you may not want to delay till the mail is sent before reporting back to the user.

```
// Send a message using the go keyword, without waiting f
or completion
message := "hello word"
go mail.Send(message, example@example.com)

// Execution continues on the main goroutine without paus
ing...
```

Waiting for go

A common failure when using goroutines in a simple program is to fail to wait for them to finish. When a program's main ends, all running goroutines that were created by the program will also be stopped. So if your main only spins up some goroutines, those goroutines may not have time to finish, and you're left waiting for godot.

```go
func main() {
    fmt.Println("waiting...")
    go func() {
    fmt.Println("godot") // doesn't arrive
    }()
}
```

waiting...

Use a wait group to make sure your goroutines are completed before the app terminates.

```go
func main() {
    var wg sync.WaitGroup
    fmt.Println("hello world")
    wg.Add(1)
    go func() {
        defer wg.Done()
        fmt.Println("goodbye, cruel world")
    }()
    wg.Wait()
}
```

hello world
goodbye, cruel world

Goroutines & range

If you range over values and launch a goroutine within your range, the value v sent to the goroutine will not change each time. . This is because the variable v is reused for each iteration of the for loop. Given a func f that prints the arguments:

```go
func f(s string) {
    fmt.Println(s)
}
```

If we run it in a goroutine, the only value printed (3 times), is the last one.

```go
values := []string{"first", "second", "last"}
for _, v := range values {
    go func() { f(v) }()
}
```

> last last last

If instead the value is passed as an argument to the goroutine function, it works as expected:

```go
for _, v := range values {
    go func(val string) { f(val) }(v)
}
```

> first second last

This is probably the most common error when using goroutines, and is easy to make as it's natural to use the values of range within the loop. Always watch for this if using a goroutine inside a for loop - some linters may warn on this.

Goroutines & Blocking functions

If you provide a blocking function as the argument to a function in a go routine, the blocking run will be run synchronously first, and the realised argument will be sent to the goroutine function.

```
// if b blocks, b will be called first, then after comple
tion f called with the result
// so b will be called before goroutine is invoked
go f(fb())
```

Instead an anonymous function could be used:

```
// b will be called in the goroutine
go func() {
  f(fb())
}()
```

Data Races

If two goroutines access the same memory without access control, this causes a race condition. Race detection is not yet automatic at compile time, but fortunately it's easy to detect at runtime with the race detector. To find data races, run your program with the -race option and it will warn you if races are detected:

```
go run -race race.go
```

An example of a data race:

```
m := make(map[string]string)

// Access OK
m["1"] = "a"

go func() {
  m["1"] = "a" // First conflicting access.
}()

m["2"] = "b" // Second conflicting access.
```

To avoid races, you can pass copies of values, or wrap access with a mutex from the sync package.

GOMAXPROCS

GOMAXPROCS sets how many processors the Go runtime uses to run goroutines on. Though it was set to 1 by default in early versions of Go for performance reasons, programs usually don't need to set GOMAXPROCS, as it is now set intelligently by the runtime based on the machine. Parallel programs might benefit from a further increase in GOMAXPROCS but be aware that concurrency is not parallelism. You may find this set in older source code, but it is very rarely necessary.

.

Channels

Channels are a queue of values of a specific type which can be used to share information safely between goroutines. You can read more about the uses of channels with goroutines in the Pipelines article on the go blog. Before using channels, consider other options, particularly if you just need to control access to shared state. You can use mutexes to control access to state across goroutines, which is much simpler than channels. Use channels to orchestrate more complex behaviour like signalling between goroutines, passing ownership of data, or distributing units of work.

Nil Channels

Sending to a nil channel blocks forever:

```go
func main() {
    var c chan string
    // send to nil channel blocks forever
    c <- "test"
}
```

Receive on a nil channel blocks forever:

```go
func main() {
    var c chan string
    // receive on nil blocks forever
    fmt.Println(<-c)
}
```

Closed Channels

Sending to a closed channel causes a panic

```
package main

import (
    "fmt"
)

func main() {
    output := make(chan int, 1)
    write(output, 2) // send
    close(output)    // close
    write(output, 3) // send after close = panic
}
```

A receive from a closed channel returns the zero value
immediately

```
package main

import "fmt"

func main() {
    c := make(chan int, 2)
    c <- 1
    c <- 2
            c <- 3
    close(c)
    for i := 0; i < 5; i++ {
        fmt.Printf("%d ", <-c)
    }
}
```

outputs the channel values then the zero value

```
1 2 0 0 0
```

Instead you can use a range loop to just get the values

```go
func main() {
    c := make(chan int, 2)
    c <- 1
    c <- 2
    close(c)
    for v := range c {
        fmt.Printf("%d ", v)
    }
}
```

Stopping a goroutine

You can use a channel to stop a goroutine by using the channel to signal completion.

```go
// create a signal channel
done := make(chan bool)

// launch the goroutine
go func() {

    // listen for signals
    for {
        select {
        case <- done:
            return
        default:
            // Do something
            // ...
        }
    }
}()

// Do something
// ...

// Stop the goroutine
done <- true
```

Deadlocks

Go channels created with make(chan T) without a size are not buffered. An unbuffered channel is synchronous, you can only send when there is a receiver. If the reads don't match the writes, the anon goroutines deadlock.

```
func main() {
    channel := make(chan string)
    done_channel := make(chan bool)
    go func() {
        channel <- "value" // write 1
        channel <- "value" // write 2
        done_channel <- true
    }()
    variable := <-channel // read 1
    ok <-done_channel
    fmt.Println(variable,ok)
}
```

fatal error: all goroutines are asleep - deadlock!

```
func main() {
    channel := make(chan string)
    done_channel := make(chan bool)
    go func() {
        channel <- "write1" // write 1
        channel <- "write2" // write 2
        done_channel <- true
    }()
    variable := <-channel // read 1
    variable = <-channel  // read 2 required to finish
    ok := <-done_channel
    fmt.Println(variable, ok)
}
```

write2 true

Counting channel elements

If you want to know how many elements are in a channel, you can just use len(channel)

```go
func main() {
    c := make(chan int, 100)
    for i := 0; i < 34; i++ {
        c <- 0
    }
    fmt.Println(len(c))
}
```

Functions & Scope

Go scope is defined by blocks. A block is a possibly empty sequence of declarations and statements within matching brace brackets. The levels of blocks are roughly:

1. Universal block - predeclared identifiers, keywords etc
2. Package block - any top level identifier outside a function
3. Function block - receivers, arguments, return values and identifiers within a function
4. Inner Blocks - identifiers declared within an inner block in a function end at the end of that block

For example package block identifiers include variables and functions within the package:

```go
// An exported variable
var Exported = "hello"

// A private variable
var pkgOnly = 1
```

Function block identifiers include receivers, arguments, return values and identifiers within a function:

```go
// Functions define a block
func (receiver T)Function(argument int) (returnValue int)
 {
    var v int
}
```

A block within a function:

```go
func (receiver T) Function(argument int) (returnValue int
) {
    var v int

    // Inner block begins
    if argument > 0 {
        var v int // shadows outer v
        v = 4 + v
    }
    // block ends

    fmt.Printf("v=%d\n", f)
    return v
}

func main() {
    T{}.Function(1)
}
```

The full rules for scope in Go are set out in the Language Spec. Blocks all create a new scope, so an if statement will start a new block, and variables declared within it will go out of scope when it ends. In contrast with Java, blocks protect their variables from the outer scope, you can overwrite a variable in the outer scope by declaring a new one in an inner scope. If required declare the variable before an if block and use it within. Otherwise Go is broadly similar to other languages in the C family, and there are few surprises here apart from shadowing variables inadvertently (see below).

Shadowing

Be careful when using the automatic assignment operator :=
that you don't accidentally shadow variables from the outer
block. In the case below err is created twice, and if you relied

on err being set in the outside scope it would not be. In most cases this isn't a problem but it's something to be aware of. Most linters warn about any dangerous instances of shadowing so if you use a linter it is not usually a problem in practice.

```go
// err is created
err := f()
if err != nil {
    // err is recreated - outer err is not updated
    v, err := f()
}
```

Defer runs after the function

The defer statement does not run at the end of a block, but at the end of the containing function.

Defer arguments are frozen

The defer statement freezes its arguments the instant it is evaluated (the line it occurs in the source code), not when it executes after leaving the containing function. This means any values changed after it occurs do not get passed to defer.

```go
// Define a string s "hello"
s := "hello"

// At point of defer, s is "hello"
defer fmt.Print(s)

// Not used, even though defer runs after
s = "hello world"
```

Switch fall through

Case statements inside a switch in go **do not fall through by default**, so break is not required. You can use the fallthrough keyword to do so if you require. This should be used sparingly and carefully annotated because of the difference with C - programmers not familiar with Go may be tripped up by it so use this sparingly if at all.

```go
switch(i) {
case 0:
// do something here
// ...
case 1:
// do something here
// ...
case 3:
    // the fallthrough keyword is required
    // to fall through explicitly
    fallthrough
default:
// do something
}
```

Naked Returns

In go, naked returns (the use of the keyword return without parameters) will return the current state of the named return values. This is sometimes used as a shortcut to avoid specifying what is returned, but has fallen somewhat out of favour. Try to avoid using naked returns in your go code, they are unclear, particularly within or at the end of a large function. Instead specify exactly what will be returned, and use nil or zero value for all values when returning an error.

Prefer synchronous functions

Try to write synchronous functions, which can then be transformed by use of the go keyword into asynchronous ones. Do not attempt to make your API async by default by using go keywords within library functions. It is easy to add concurrency with the go keyword, but impossible to remove it if a function uses it internally.

Prefer functions over methods

Coming from an object-oriented background, many programmers reach for structs and methods first. Before using a method, you should consider whether you could instead use a function. Functions are independent of the data they work with, and ideally use their inputs and no other state, so that the output is predictable. Use a method where you need to reflect the state of the type the method is attached to.

Packages

In Go packages are a way of scoping code, and map exactly to folders. Within a package, code can refer to any identifier within that package, public or private, while those importing the package may only reference public identifiers beginning with an uppercase letter. Each package can contain multiple Go files, and each Go file in a package begins with a declaration at the top of the file for the form:

```
// Package x ... this comment explains succinctly what th
e package does
package x
```

where x is the package name. The name should be short, explicit and avoid punctuation - see Package Names on the Go blog. The line preceding the package declaration can be used to document the package - typically this will be done in the most important file in the package, the one which has the same name as the package itself.

Packages vs Dirs

Packages are a directory on the file system containing .go files. **You cannot have multiple packages within one directory**. By convention, the package name is the same as the directory name, and the directory should contain a file of the package name with the .go suffix which contains the primary exports. You can if necessary rename packages on import and use a different package name to the folder name.

Workspaces

A common cause of confusion for beginners with Go is the concept of workspaces, where all your go code lives. These are not checked into version control directly, and when beginning you will just have one workspace which is your gopath. This contains three dirs src, pkg, and bin, as detailed in the getting started section. Projects will typically be hosted under paths like this: src/host/username/project which are used as the import paths, and below that path can contain any directories you want to structure your project.

Project structure

There are few restrictions on structure in a Go project, but for a beginner there are a few guidelines to keep in mind. The simplest structure is one main package at the top level of your repository. This can be fetched by go get which is what users will expect. Beyond this you can structure it as you wish, with as many directories as you wish, though each directory with go files must be a separate package, and cannot contain more than one package.

A few guidelines to live by:

- Make your project go-gettable by having the main package at the top level
- Err on the side of fewer packages, not more
- Import lower packages from higher levels, and try to avoid interdependencies - low level packages should stand alone
- Store internal libraries not for export in a directoy named

internal
- Vendor dependencies in a top level directory named vendor
- Always flatten vendor directories into this one top level folder

Packages can contain as many files as you want, not just one, and typically should be split by file. Don't split packages by type and have one type per package, a package will normall contain several types.

Blank imports

You can import packages with the blank identifier solely for their init function, to do this prefix the import with _

```
import _ "net/http/pprof"
```

This makes it clear the package is unused but the init function will be called (which may introduce side effects in this case registering handlers).

Don't import main

You should never try to import the main package. Always try to import from the top level down, so your lowest level packages know nothing about the levels above. This is not always possible but is a good guideline – avoid a fragile web of dependencies between internal packages which makes your program harder to reason about - prefer some copying to interdependent packages.

Cyclic dependencies

If you run into cyclic imports, you have a package A which imports package B which then imports package A. To avoid this, try to keep your imports in one direction, importing small packages into the top level one. For example for a git command line tool you might have a main command, which imported a package which contains all the git specific structures and could be used as a library by that command, a server or any other type of app. The git package should never know about packages which import it.

If you structure your apps this way you will avoid cyclic imports and you should consider them a hint that something is wrong with your design.

Using goimports

If you choose to use goimports instead of go fmt on save, and have several packages with the same name at different places in your GOPATH , it may not choose the correct imports, or even those closest to the importing package.

There is a fix almost ready for this, but that leaves the problem of imports from third party packages which might be replaced by an import from another package with the same name and similar code by mistake. So if you use the goimports tool use it with caution and always check the imports inserted - it chooses the shortest name by default and may import an unexpected package if you have homonym packages under gopath.

Using go get

You should be aware that go get fetches the most recent version of any go package. This means if you are sharing code and want reproducible builds, you need to use the vendor directory. In practice because of the Go culture of no breaking changes this is rarely a problem, but sometimes APIs change, and this can lead to subtle breakage in your program if you are not careful. Try to vendor any dependencies you don't control to avoid this problem.

Vendoring packages

There is no official package manager tool as yet in Go, though work is progressing on one (go dep). For now you can vendor your packages inside a vendor directory in your project, and those imports will be used instead of the imports currently. You can read more about this behaviour in the go command documentation under Vendor Directories.

Internal directories

A subdirectory named 'internal' can be used for packages that can only be imported by nearby code, not by any other package. Packages in an internal directory are only accessible to those in the same file tree, rooted at the parent of the internal directory. So if one project includes 'myproj/example/internal/foo' only packages under myproj can import foo.

This is typically used for dependencies which should not be shared and are for internal use only (for example libraries with an unstable api).

Don't import unsafe

If you can, avoid using the unsafe or reflect packages in your code – this also applies to libraries you import. Package unsafe bypasses the Go type system. Packages that import unsafe may be non-portable and are not protected by the Go 1 compatibility guidelines.

Don't import reflect

Package reflect also bypasses the Go type system, so programs using it don't have the benefit of strict type checks, programs that use it will typically be slower and more fragile, and may use interface{} too much. It can be temping when writing a library to use reflect and attempt to handle several types in the same function (for example an array of types or a single type), but this makes it confusing for users (no indication of what type should be passed in), and easy to miss a type and cause panics.

```go
// Think twice!
import "reflect"

// Using reflect and empty interfaces
// obscures your intent for callers
// and subverts the type system
func MyAPIFunc(myvar interface{}) {
    // ... requires typecasts and perhaps reflect
}
```

Cgo is not Go

Cgo is a useful crutch to allow calling into C libraries from Go and vice versa. Build times will be slower, and you won't be able to cross compile code easily. This throws away many of the advantages of writing code in Go. You can use it to do some very useful things like running Go programs on iOS or Android, or interfacing with large libraries of existing code written in C, and it is indispensable for those uses, but if you can avoid using it, do so.

Syscall and cgo are not portable

If you're using cgo or syscall, your package probably isn't portable, and needs build tags for each platform you're going to target. Unlike other packages in the go ecosystem, the cgo or syscall packages are not portable across platforms. If you import them, you should be aware of this.

Init funcs

Packages can contain (one or several) init() functions to set up state, these are run after all the imports and package variables have been initialised:

```
// init() loads the configuration for this package
func init() {
  if user == "" {
        log.Fatal("$USER not set")
  }
  if home == "" {
    home = "/home/" + user
  }
}
```

Avoid using this if you can, and particularly avoid using it to set global state (like set flags in other packages, or attach handlers to the http.DefaultServeMux) - doing so can lead to subtle bugs. The init function should be solely concerned with the package it is in.

Flags

Libraries and packages should not define their own flags or use the flags package. Instead take parameters to define behaviour - the application (main) should be in charge of parsing flags and passing the chosen configuration values in to a package. Otherwise it will be difficult to reuse the package or import it anywhere else.

Interfaces

An interface in go is a contract specifying which method signatures a type must have. Crucially, it is specified by the user of the interface, not the code which satisfies it.

Keep interfaces simple

> The bigger the interface, the weaker the abstraction – Rob Pike

Interfaces are at their most powerful when they express a simple contract that any type can easily conform to. If they start to demand a laundry list of functions (*more than a few* is a good rule of thumb), they have very little advantage over a concrete type as an argument, because the caller is not going to be able to create an alternative type without substantially recreating the original.

Here are some examples of useful interfaces from the standard library, you'll notice that all of these extremely popular interfaces have one thing in common - they all require very few functions.

error

Error represents an error condition, and only returns a string with a description of the error.

```
type error interface {
    Error() string
}
```

fmt.Stringer

Used when formatting values for fmt.Printf and friends.

```go
type Stringer interface {
        String() string
}
```

io.Reader

Read reads len(p) bytes from the data stream.

```go
type Reader interface {
        Read(p []byte) (n int, err error)
}
```

io.Writer

Write writes len(p) bytes from p to a data .stream.

```go
type Writer interface {
        Write(p []byte) (n int, err error)
}
```

http.ResponseWriter

HTTP handlers are passed a ResponseWriter to write the HTTP response to a request.

```
type ResponseWriter interface {
        // Header returns the header map used to set head
ers.
        Header() Header

        // Write writes the data to the connection as par
t of an HTTP reply.
        Write([]byte) (int, error)

        // WriteHeader writes an HTTP response header wit
h just a status code - used for errors.
        WriteHeader(int)
}
```

Avoid the empty Interface

The empty interface is written like this, but unlike most interfaces it requires no methods (hence the empty brackets):

```
interface{}
```

It is the equivalent of:

```
type MyInterface interface {
}
```

Don't overuse empty interface - *it means nothing*. If you find yourself using empty interface and then switching on type, consider instead defining separate functions which operate on concrete types. Don't try to use empty interface as a poor man's generics - it is possible, but it subverts the type system and makes it very easy to cause panics.

Accept interfaces, return types

Interfaces are a way of avoiding tight coupling between different packages, so they are most useful when defined at their point of use, and only used there. If you export an interface as a return type, you are forcing others to use this interface only forever, or to attempt to cast your interface back into a concrete type.

Do not design interfaces for mocking, design them for real world use, and don't add methods to them before you have a concrete use for the methods. The exception to this is of course the extremely common error interface.

Avoid mixing interface and concrete types

When defining interfaces in a package, don't also provide the implementation in the same package, because the receiver should define interfaces, not the implementer – you may sometimes need to break this guideline.

- Define interfaces in the package that uses them
- Define concrete types in the package that uses the package that accepts an interface

Don't use pointers to interface

You probably meant to use a pointer to your real type, or just a plain old Interface. You don't need a pointer to interfaces.

Don't compare interface to nil

An interface will only be nil when both their type and value fields are nil, so comparing interface to nil can have unexpected results. Don't do that. You can read more about this problem in the, but in summary if any concrete value has ever been stored in the interface, the interface will not be nil.

```go
// E is a type conforming to the error interface
type E struct{}
func (e *E) Error() string { return fmt.Sprintf("%p", e) }

// typederror returns an interface
func typederror() error {
    var e *E = nil
    return e // e is not nil as expected
}
```

You can read more about the internals of interfaces in Go Data Structures: Interfaces on Russ Cox's blog.

Writing Servers in Go

When writing servers in go, you'll probably make extensive
use of the standard library.The net and net/http packages are
some of the most widely used in the Go ecosystem, and
come with some unique pitfalls. The source to the net/http
package is surprisingly straightforward and readable, and if
you're going to write servers, you should read through the
docs and the source of this package at least once to see
what is available.

Getting Started

Running a simple server is drop-dead simple in Go, and to
get started all you need is a handlerFunc as the http package
contains a default router and server you can use. A Handler
in go is a function which responds to http requests, usually for
a specific route on your server (thought they can be general,
like an error handler or a static file handler). It is a very simple
function with two arguments: the Request, and an
http.ResponseWriter to write a response to. Except for
reading the body, handlers should not modify the provided
Request.

```go
// A handler function in go reads the request
// and writes a response to the ResponseWriter
func HelloServer(w http.ResponseWriter, req *http.Request
) {
    io.WriteString(w, "hello, world!\n")
}

func main() {
    // Attach our handler function to the default mux
    http.HandleFunc("/hello", HelloServer)

    // Ask the http package to start a server
    // on port 8080 (note the port is a string)
    err := http.ListenAndServe(":8080", nil)
    if err != nil {
        log.Fatal(err)
    }
}
```

Handlers

When writing handlers, be aware that the http.Request.Body is an io.ReadCloser, which means it doesn't have to be read into memory all at once, but can be read as a stream. Consider using the io.Reader interface if you need to pass it to a decoder or receive large requests. The request Body will always be non-nil, and the server will close it, so handlers do not need to.

Similarly, the http.ResponseWriter is an io.Writer, so it can be written to in a stream, and io.Copy can be used to read from one source and write it to the output (for example when reading a file) without reading everything into a buffer first.

Try to use these interfaces if possible when reading from requests and writing responses.

Servers

You normally should not use the http.DefaultServeMux, in case other packages have decided to register handlers on it, and you expose those handlers without knowing about it. For example the pprof package by default will install handlers simply by being imported.

Also set the timeouts on your server explicitly to sensible defaults as the default timeouts are not advisable, but cannot be changed because of the Go 1 promise. You can read more about these timeouts in the complete guide to net/http timeouts and So you want to expose go on the internet by @filosottile at cloudflare. If you're interested in networking, the cloudflare blog has a lot of good articles on Go.

```
// Setting up your own server,
// specifying some default timeouts
srv := &http.Server{
    ReadTimeout:  5 * time.Second,
    WriteTimeout: 10 * time.Second,
    IdleTimeout:  120 * time.Second,
    TLSConfig:    tlsConfig,
    // Always set the router to avoid using http.DefaultS
erveMux
    // which is accessible to all other packages
    Handler:      serveMux,
}
log.Println(srv.ListenAndServeTLS("", ""))
```

Implicit goroutines

The http server uses goroutines to run your handlers and serve multiple requests in parallel, so **each handler is in a new goroutine**. This means you have to be careful about sharing memory between handlers. If for example you have a global config struct or cache, this must be protected by a mutex. Always run your server programs with a race tester to catch bugs like this as they can creep in if you are not vigilant about finding them.

Listen and Serve Blocks

If you launch the http server in your main goroutine, don't expect control to return to your main function until the end of the program, because it blocks waiting for input until an error occurs.

```go
func main() {
    http.HandleFunc("/hello", HelloServer)
    err := http.ListenAndServe(":12345", nil)
    if err != nil {
        log.Fatal(err)
    }
    log.Println("this line will never execute")
}
```

Serving Files

Don't perform **any** file operations on paths before you clean them, and root them at a known good path. If you're serving an entire directory of files, consider using http.FileServer instead of http.ServeFile:

```go
fileServer := http.FileServer(http.Dir("./public/static")
)
http.Handle("/static/", http.StripPrefix("/static", fileS
erver))
```

If you are using os.Stat, ioutil.ReadAll, or http.ServeFile or similar functions with user input (be that in the request url or params), be sure to sanitise the file path first, and root it at a known public path. The default mux will usually strip .. from urls before presenting to handlers and ServeFile has some protections against directory traversal, but it is better to be very careful when accessing local files based on anything from user input.

If you wish to serve static content but present a custom 404 page to users, set up a file handler which checks if files exist and returns 404 or 401 in case of problems accessing the file, but otherwise calls ServeFile.

```
// Clean the path and prefix with our public dir
localPath := "./public" + path.Clean(r.URL.Path)

// Check the file exists
s, err := os.Stat(localPath)
if err != nil {
    // If file not found return 404 page
    if os.IsNotExist(err) {
        renderNotFound()
        return
    }

    // For other file errors render unauthorised and retu
rn
    http.Error(w, "Not Authorized", http.StatusUnauthoriz
ed)
    return
}

// If not a file return 404 page
if s.IsDir() {
    renderNotFound()
    return
}

// Serve the file content
http.ServeFile(w, r, localPath)
```

Bad Requests

The built in Go server will reject bad requests before they hit
your handlers, so you will never see them. It will return a
code 400 Bad Request to the client. There is at present no
way to override this. Normally this isn't a problem but it's
something to be aware of. For example this bad request
using curl to hit a local go server would never hit your
handlers:

```
# Perform an invalid request using curl
curl http://localhost:3000/%3
```

and would simply return to the client:

400 Bad Request

If your go server is behind a proxy like nginx or a load balancer those will also intercept such requests.

Panics in goroutines

If a handler panics, the server assumes that the panic was isolated to the current request, recovers, logs a stack trace to the server log, and closes the connection. So the server will recover from any panics in your handlers, but if your handlers use the go keyword, they must protect against panics **within any separate** goroutines they create, otherwise those goroutines can crash the entire server with a panic. See the errors chapter for more details.

One approach to this problem is never to make mistakes. However with unpredictable, malformed or downright malicious data coming from outside the application in parameters or files this can be difficult, so it may be worth protecting against panics in any goroutines launched from your handlers.

Cryptography

If you're trying to work with cryptography in go, definitely view this talk from George Tankersley at CoreOS on Crypto for Go developers, which comes with cryptopasta example code.

Random Numbers

If generating random numbers for a server, you probably want them to be unpredictable, so use crypto/rand, not math/rand.

```go
// Example by George Tankersley
// NewEncryptionKey generates a random 256-bit key
// for Encrypt() and Decrypt().
// It panics if the source of randomness fails.
func NewEncryptionKey() *[32]byte {
    key := [32]byte{}
    _, err := io.ReadFull(rand.Reader, key[:])
    if err != nil {
        panic(err)
    }
    return &key
}
```

Comparing Passwords

If you're comparing passwords or other sensitive data, to avoid timing attacks, make use of the crypto/subtle subtle.ConstantTimeCompare, or better still use the bcrypt package library functions bcrypt.CompareHashAndPassword.

Cookies

Cookies are just headers passed between client and server, so they're not complex, but go provides some utilities for manipulating them. The server sends cookies with SetCookie on the http.ResponseWriter (not on the request). NB that invalid cookies may be silently dropped when set or received.

If you want to use cookies with invalid values including strings like space or @, you will need to use your own cookie implementation.

```go
// handler sets a cookie on the request
func handler(w http.ResponseWriter, r *http.Request) {
    cookie := http.Cookie{
        // Set the name
        Name:    "session_name",
        // Set a value on the cookie
        Value:   "cookie_value",
        // Always set the domain
        Domain:  "example.com",
        // Always set the path
        Path:    "/",
        // Optional expiry time
        Expires: time.Now().AddDate(1, 0, 0),
        // MaxAge=0 means no Max-Age
        MaxAge:  0,
        // Allow only the server to access the cookie
        HttpOnly: true,
        // Set this if using https
        Secure:   true,
    }
    // Set the cookie on the response
    http.SetCookie(w, &cookie)
    // Write the rest of the response
    w.WriteHeader(http.StatusOK)
    io.WriteString(w, "hello")
}
```

If you want to store information in cookies you should try to keep it limited, and encrypt the information stored, as it is stored on the client machine outside your control.

The gorilla/sessions package allows you to use encrypted cookies and store session-specific information.

Making http requests

Your program may need to fetch http resources, and the net/http package offers http.Get or http.Client in order to help with this, but there are some issues you should be aware of.

Client Timeouts

The http client has no default timeout, which can be a problem. In this example problem the client waits 10 minutes before exiting.

```go
package main
import (
  "fmt"
  "net/http"
  "net/http/httptest"
  "time"
)
func main() {
  svr := httptest.NewServer(http.HandlerFunc(func(w http.
ResponseWriter, r *http.Request) {
    // handler sleeps for 10 minutes
    time.Sleep(10 * time.Minute)
  }))
  defer svr.Close()

  // Make a get request with default client
  fmt.Println("making request")
  http.Get(svr.URL)
  fmt.Println("finished request")
}
```

Instead, you should create a client explicitly with a timeout:

```
// Create a client with a timeout of 10 seconds
var netClient = &http.Client{
  Timeout: time.Second * 10,
}
response, _ := netClient.Get(url)
```

Closing the response body

Don't close the response body before you check if there was
an error.

```
r, err := http.Get("https://example.com")
// Don't defer close here
if err != nil {
  return err
}
// It's safe to defer close
// once you know there was no error
defer r.Body.Close()
```

Accepting uploads

If accepting uploads via a multipart form, be aware that temp
files created will not be automatically deleted by Go. You
should therefore delete them with Request.Form.RemoveAll
after they have been used by the server.

Check Status Codes

Always check the status code of the response when making a
request with the Go http client. If the status is in the 200
range you can use the response as is. If it is in the 300 range
it is a redirection. If it is in the 400 range you have a problem

with your request which you should fix (e.g. invalid headers, invalid URL). If it is in the 500 range there was a problem on the server end, so you need to inform the user.

The error returned by http.Get and friends informs you if there was an error reading the response, not if the response was successful.

```
url := "https://example.com"
resp, err := http.Get(url)
if err != nil {
    return fmt.Errorf("error getting %s: %v",url,err)
}

// Unexpected response, inform the user
if resp.StatusCode < 200 || resp.StatusCode > 299 {
    return fmt.Errorf("unexpected http status:%d",resp.St
atusCode)
}

// No errors fetching, so the response is ok to use
```

Utilities

Under the net/http package are several utility packages which make life easier when debugging or testing http Requests.

In particular, the httputil package provides:

httputil.DumpRequest

DumpRequest outputs a nicely formatted version of the request passed to it, making the request content much clearer.

httputil.DumpResponse

DumpResponse outputs a nicely formatted version of the response passed to it, making the response content much clearer.

httputil.ReverseProxy

Provides a simple reverse proxy handler

And the httptest package provides several useful functions and types:

httptest.NewRequest

Provides a new request suitable for sending to a Handler for testing.

httptest.ResponseRecorder

ResponseRecorder is a ResponseWriter which records the response data written by a handler so that it can be compared in tests to the expected response.

Profiling

The http/pprof package provides excellent support for profiling your server, and can be used to generate data for use in flame graphs or other graphical representations of your program.

To use it, simply import the package:

```
import _ "net/http/pprof"
```

Beware though if you register it there are hidden side effects. The pprof package will attach endpoints to the default serve mux during init, but unfortunately this behaviour cannot change due to the Go 1 promise. For this and performance reasons you should not import it in production, but use it for development only. You can find out more about profiling in Profiling Go Programs.

Latency

When optimising servers it's worth being aware of the comparative times for operations. If your database is in a different data centre for example on another continent, it doesn't matter how optimised your code is if it needs to spend 150ms for every database request.

1 CPU cycle takes 0.0000003ms, Cache access 0.0000129ms, Solid state disk 0.05ms, Rotational disk access around 1ms and on internet request around 200ms across continents. So make sure you're optimising the right operations - avoiding network access will always be faster than any other optimisation.

Templates

The Go Standard Library offers templating of both text and html content. The html templates offer a superset of the text template features, including contextual escaping, but the interface can be a little confusing.

The missing docs

There is extensive documentation of the template packages, but most of it is in the text/template package, not the html/template package, so be sure to read that as well, even if you intend to focus on using html/template. The html template package extends the text/template package and uses much of its functionality, so you need to read the documentation for both.

Delimiters

If you have problems with the go template delimiters clashing with other libraries, you can use the Delims function in order to set the delimiters to some other string. Note this must be done first, before files are parsed:

```go
// Set the delimiters on this template
tmpl, err := template.New("").Delims("[[", "]]").ParseFil
es("foo.tmpl", "bar.tmpl")
```

Dot

The dot character in go templates represents the data context, and is set on Execution. Within functions like range the dot is set within that scope to the successive elements of the array. To access the parent context within a range use `$.`.

Inline templates

While normally templates are complex enough to require their own files, you may find it useful to define templates as strings inline in your go code, particularly if sharing them on the playground. When templates are over a few lines this can become cumbersome and you might want to consider storing them in files and reading them in to a template set.

```go
// Define a simple template to print data
inline := `Hello, {{.}}`

// Set data to the string world!
data := `world!`

// Load the template
t, err := template.New("t").Parse(inline)
if err != nil {
    panic(err)
}

// Print the template 't' to stdout
// using data as the context
err = t.ExecuteTemplate(os.Stdout, "t", data)
```

Prints the template "Hello, " + the data "world!"

Hello, world!

Escaping

The Go template package assumes that template authors (and by extension the templates) are trusted, but that the data inserted into the template is not. The HTML templates offer contextual escaping, so the package knows about the structure of html and the context in which data is escaped matters - the same data inside a url, an attribute or text content may be escaped differently.

For example the text "O'Reilly & co" is escaped differently depending on whether it is found inside script tags, an attribute or an href attribute.

```
tmpl := `Hello, <a class="{{.}}" href="{{.}}"> {{.}}<
/a><script>{{.}}</script>`
data := `O'Reilly >`

// Load the template
t, err := template.New("t").Parse(tmpl)
if err != nil {
    panic(err)
}

// Execute the template
err = t.ExecuteTemplate(os.Stdout, "t", data)
```

```
Hello, <a class="O&#39;Reilly &amp; co"
href="O%27Reilly%20&amp;%20co"> O&#39;Reilly &amp; co</a>
<script>"O'Reilly \u0026 co"</script>
```

If you need to bypass escaping, you can use the appropriate typed string like template.HTML in a function or field, to indicate to the package that this is trusted content. Be very careful not to use user content in such cases, or to escape it properly before use.

Structs, fields and methods

There is a uniform interface for fields and methods of a struct - the . operator will call either a field or a method. The same is true of map entries. You can also use the built-in function index to access members of Maps and Slices.

```
{{ index mymap 0 }}
```

Func Maps

Templates have a set of global functions available, which are documented in the text/template package, these offer logical operations, printing and a few other conveniences.

To extend these Templates offer a FuncMap, which allows you to add functions to templates if you need to format data in a particular way (for example formatting currencies), or provide global data like the title of your website or string translations without threading it through all the different handlers and setting it explicitly as part of the data provided to templates. Don't get too carried away adding functions to your templates though - they are deliberately pared down version of go so that most of the logic resides in your .go files, rather than in template files, and to keep the attack surface to a minimum. Templates are deliberately minimalist in Go and you should strive to keep them so.

Prefix operators

The boolean operators available in templates are all
functions, which means they use prefix notation. Use *and* x y,
not x *and* y. If you're coming from Ruby this may come as a
surprise, as using *and* with one argument will appear to work,
but does not behave as you might expect.

```
{{/* Don't do this, it will always be true if x is non ni
l */}}
{{ if x and y}}

{{ end }}

{{/* Do this instead */}}
{{ if and x y}}

{{ end }}
```

Range functions

Go templates also allow you to range, but unlike the range in
Go code, using this function with one argument yields the
value, not the index.

```
{{ $v := range .values }}
```

There are numerous small differences between Go templates
and Go code like this, so don't assume that the template
language reflects Go norms.

Writing comma separated lists

If using range in templates to write a list, which must be comma separated (JSON for example requires commas on all array items, but not the last), the neatest way to do this is to use if $i immediately after the range call:

```
// Print ',' before every element but the first one
{{ $i, $v := range .values }}{{if $i}}, {{end}}
<a href="/{{.}}"> {{.}} </a>
{{ end }}
```

Printing values

The printf function is available in templates to print values as strings:

```
{{ printf "%s %d %d" "hello" 1 1 }}
```

The line eater

If you need to add newlines in your template for legibility (for example when outputting many columns of csv), you can invoke the line eater with the - symbol beside the braces (either start or end braces). The template:

```
{{- .One }}
{{- .Two -}}
```

will output the values with whitespace removed:

foobar

Template Sets

There are several different ways to define templates and name them - they can be named inline in the template, or named by one of the ParseFiles or ParseGlob functions, or named on creation with template.New("t"). If using ParseGlob you'd have to make sure the file names used are always unique, which can be problematic in a large project. Another approach is to use the relative path of template files as the name, to ensure uniqueness, and make it clear when reading templates which file on disk is being included.

Templates can only include to those in the same set, so you may find it convenient to load all templates into the same set with distinct names (perahps using the location of the templates loaded) so that they can be pulled in to any template by path.

Rendering Nested Templates

To render a template within another template, assuming they are in the same set, use the template function, which takes the name of the content to place, and the data context to render it with (use the dot operator to obtain the current context).

```
<body>
<h1>Hello</h1>
{{ template "views/users/content.html.got" . }}
</body>
```

This will render the template with name "views/users/content.html.got" inside the main template above.

Template Blocks

Template blocks, introduced in Go 1.6, can be used to define areas of a template to replace with other content by overlaying it with another template. The master template should be created as normal, then Clone used to copy it with an overlay template. This may seem counter-intuitive at first.

Another approach to achieve a similar result is to create a layout template with a `.content` key, which can then have content (itself rendered from a separate template) inserted into it using this key.

```
<body>
<h1>Hello</h1>
{{block "content" .}}
<p>Default content</p>
{{ end }}
</body>
```

Databases

If you're unsure which database to use, Postgresql is a highly reliable, well maintained project and has excellent drivers for Go. the examples shown below use psql, but can be adapted for other databases. Go has drivers for all the mainstream databases, as well as a selection of time series and key/value stores written in Go.

You can find a list of go database drivers on the Go wiki page SQL Drivers - prefer a driver which doesn't use cgo and conforms to the database/sql interface if possible.

Importing a driver

Importing a database driver is used to register the database driver. In retrospect this is an unfortunate design decision, and it would be better to register drivers explicitly, but it won't change in Go 1. So import the driver as follows in order to register it and use a given database:

```
import (
  "database/sql"
  // This line registers the database driver
  // and exposes the standard database/sql interface
  _ "github.com/lib/pq"
)
```

If code imports lots of drivers, it will be importing all the code, and registering the drivers on init, so only import those you need to use in a program. If importing drivers with the blank identifier as above you can only use the standard sql interface defined in database/sql. You may find you want to use a higher level package to simplify common operations, or write your own wrapper for the database in complex applications.

Opening a connection

When you open a connection to the database, you must ping it to ensure it opened correctly

```
// Open the database (no connection is miade)
db, err := sql.Open("postgres","postgres://azurediamond:h
unter2@localhost/azurediamond?sslmode=verify-full")
        "user:password@tcp(127.0.0.1:3306)/hello")
if err != nil {
    return err
}


// Check the db connection
err = db.Ping()
if err != nil {
    return err
}
```

Closing a connection

Don't close the connection to the database frequently as it is designed to be recycled, you should ideally create one connection per datastore which lasts for the lifetime of your application. For example you might call defer db.Close in main.

```
defer db.Close()
```

Querying the database

Querying the database can be driver specific, especially for more advanced features, so be sure to read the driver documentation for the particular database/sql flavour you're using.

Parameter placeholders

The different databases use different formats for parameter placeholders, for example they don't all support ? as you might expect. The Mysql driver uses ?, ? etc, the sqlite driver uses ?, ? etc , the Postgresql driver uses $1, $2 etc and the Oracle driver uses :val1, :val2 etc. Sqlx is one of the few drivers to support named query parameters.

Reading values

To read Values from the database, use db.Query to fetch a result:

```
// Select from the db
sql := "select count from users where status=100"
rows, err := db.Query(sql)
if err != nil {
    return err
}
defer rows.Close()
```

And rows.Scan to scan in the rows received back:

```
// Read the count (just one row and one col)
var count int
for rows.Next() {
    err = rows.Scan(&count)
    if err != nil {
      return err
    }
}
```

Reading a Row into a struct

To read a single row into a struct, you can use Query Row. You may want to add a constructor to your models which takes a row and instantiates the model from it, but the code below is a minimal example.

```
// Query a row from the database
row := db.QueryRow("select id,name,created_at from tablen
ame where id=?", id)

type Resource struct{
    ID int
    Name string
    CreatedAt time.Time
}
var r Resource
err := row.Scan(&r.ID, &r.Name, &r.CreatedAt) // This ass
umes no values are nil in the database
if err != nil {
    return err
}
```

Scanning into a struct

Many database libraries use reflect to attempt to introspect struct fields. You should try to avoid using reflect if you can as it is slow, prone to panics, and requires you to use struct tags and a dsl invented by the database library author. Another approach is to generate a list of columns, and pass them to the struct itself to assign, since it knows all about its fields and which values should go into them. This will require the struct to validate the column values and deal with nulls.

```go
type User struct {
    ID int
    Name string
    CreatedAt time.Time
}

func ReadUser(columns map[string]interface{}) *User {
    u := &User{}
    u.ID = validateInt(cols["id"])
    u.Name = validateString(cols["name"])
    u.CreatedAt = validateTime(cols["created_at"])
    return u
}
```

Handling Relations

This can seem a bit more fiddly than other languages, however the best approach is a straightforward one - retrieve the indexes of relations, and then if you require all of their information, retrieve the relations separately from the database.

You can of course retrieve them with a join at the same time, but in complex apps it helps to separate retrieving relations from retrieving the actual relation records, which is often not necessary (for example you might need to know a user has 8 images, and which ids they have, but not all the image captions and image data). Being forced to handle relations manually does have advantages compared to the say ActiveRecord which can pull in far too much data behind the scenes.

Connections are recycled

Database connections may be called from many goroutines and connections are pooled by the driver. So don't use stateful sql commands like USE, BEGIN or COMMIT, LOCK TABLES etc and instead use the facilities offered by the sql driver. There's no default limit on the number of connections, so it is possible to exhaust the number of connections allowed by the database. You can use SetMaxOpenConns and SetMaxIdleConns to control this behaviour.

```
db.SetMaxIdleConns(10)
db.SetMaxOpenConns(100)
```

Null values

If your database may contain null values, you must guard against them. One way to do this is to scan into a map of empty interface and then assert that the interface{} contains the type you (as opposed to a special null value). If it fails, use the zero value of the type instead.

Getting Database columns

If you wish to know which columns are in a row, you can call:

```
// Get a list of column names for the row
cols, err := rows.Columns()
```

This might be useful if you vary selects (e.g. sometimes select just id and created at, sometimes select the full model), and yet wish to always use a standard constructor for models which can be passed a map[string]interface{} with the values.

Writing to the database

```
// Insert a row
row := db.QueryRow("insert into tablename VALUES($1,$2,$3
)", args...)
// Retrieve the inserted id
err = row.Scan(&id)
// Return the id and any error
return id, err
```

Multiple Statements

The database/sql interface doesn't specify that drivers should support multiple statements, which means the behaviour is undefined and it's probably best to send single statements, unless your driver explicitly supports it.

Time in Go

Go includes a good set of primitives for dealing with time in the standard library. There are a few oddities detailed below.

Time on Go Playground

The playground starts with the same time for every run to make sure output is deterministic, so examples including time may not function as you expect on the playground. For more details see Inside the Go Playground..

Time Formatting

Datetime formatting in Go is rather unusual. It uses a format string which also functions as an example time; unfortunately in practice this is rather difficult to remember. The Parse and Format functions take this format layout:

```
Mon Jan 2 15:04:05 -0700 MST 2006
```

the default time format for dates is and the time package uses the memorable constant `time.RFC3339` for timestamps in international date format ISO 8601:

```
"2006-01-02T15:04:05Z07:00"
```

You may want to define some constants for any date formats you normally use, to avoid constantly referring to the time package, for example:

```
const (
    Date     = "2006-01-02"
    DateTime = "2006-01-02 15:04"
)
```

AddDate

The AddDate function adjusts dates according to arbitrary overflow rules to ensure that results are reversible. If adding Years or days, the results will generally be as expected, but if adding months, the results may not be as users expect and does not match the output of popular programs like excel.

For example subtracting one month from October 31 yields October 1st

```
// Oct 31st minus 1 month is Oct 1st,
// not Sept 30th according to Go
input := time.Date(2016, 10, 31, 0, 0, 0, 0, time.UTC)
output := time.Date(2016, 9, 30, 0, 0, 0, 0, time.UTC)
result := input.AddDate(0, -1, 0)
if result != output {
    fmt.Printf("got:%v want:%v\n", result, output)
}
```

The results will be unpredictable and depend on the day chosen and the number of days in the target month. If the number of days of the start month and the end month do not match, results can be unexpected. This is important if your users expect to add 9 months and 1 day to a given date to conform with accounting rules for example - typically this means 9 calendar months without rollover and then 1 day to be added. There is no way round this except writing your own code to handle adding months in a more predictable way.

Time Zones

You should **strongly** prefer to store times as **UTC**, and convert them for display. This makes comparisons and calculations straightforward, and allows you to customise display for the user's current location at the time of viewing. When creating times or comparing with the current time, always use the t.UTC() function to be sure you compare the UTC time.

If you need to convert times, you can convert times from a given zone to a location easily enough:

```go
// Load a set location
l, err := time.LoadLocation("America/Mexico_City")

// Set the time zone
now := t.In(l)
```

Monotonic time

Since `Go 1.9`, the time package now transparently tracks monotonic time in each Time value, making computing durations between two Time values a safe operation in the presence of wall clock adjustments.

If Times t and u both contain monotonic clock readings, the operations t.After(u), t.Before(u), t.Equal(u), and t.Sub(u) are carried out using the monotonic clock readings alone, ignoring the wall clock readings. If either t or u contains no monotonic clock reading, these operations fall back to using the wall clock readings.

Times may not contain a monotonic clock reading if they pass through functions like AddDate Round or Truncate, or if they come from parsed external sources, so don't assume they always will have.

Comparing time

When comparing time you should usually use the Time.Equal method rather than ==, as the == operator also compares both Location, which sets the time zone offset but not the absolute time, and the monotonic clock reading, which can be stripped in some circumstances.

In general, prefer t.Equal(u) to t == u, since t.Equal uses the most accurate comparison available and correctly handles the case when only one of its arguments has a monotonic clock reading.

```
t := time.Now()
t2 := time.Now().UTC()
if t.Equal(t2) {
    // Use t.Equal to compare times
}
```

Formats vs Values

Time

Despite their beguiling appearance, time formats are not time values, so if testing parsing, be aware that using a format as a value is often invalid due to formatting directives in the format string which are not valid in a time:

```go
// Time formats are not always valid values
_, err := time.Parse(time.RFC3339, time.RFC3339)
fmt.Println("error", err) // RFC3339 is not a valid time
```

error parsing time "2006-01-02T15:04:05Z07:00": extra text: 07:00

Errors & Logging

Errors and logging are one area of Go which does perhaps does deserve the label of simplistic rather than simple. The log package has no levels or interfaces, it simply prints to standard error by default. For many applications though, this is enough, and there are various logging packages available for more sophisticated requirements. The error type is very simple and errors are stored as strings.

The Error Type

Errors are values – Rob Pike

The error type in go is a very simple interface, with one method. Errors offer no introspection into what went wrong or storage of other data. Often errors are nested, as one error may be annotated several times as it passes up the stack. Try to prefer handling an error as close to the site of the error as possible.

```
type error interface {
  Error() string
}
```

You can use your own type for error, as long as it conforms to this interface, in some cases you might want to use a more complex type than the string only errors favoured by the standard library, to record an http status code for example.

If you're defining interfaces, prefer requiring the error interface rather than a concrete type. You can use type assertions to determine if an error is of the type you're interested in.

to, err := human()

to, err := human() – Francesc Campoy

The convention in Go code is always to return an error as the last argument of a function, so if it has multiple arguments. Return an error as the last argument, and try to make it as specific as possible:

```
func DoSomething() error {
    to, err := human()
    if err != nil [
      // Annotate the error and return
      return fmt.Errorf("pkgname: failed to human %s",err
)
    }
    // no, error, use value to
    ...
    return nil // return nil error
}
```

```
func DoSomethingElse() (value, value, error) {
  ...
  if err != nil {
  // Annotate the error and return nil value + error
    return nil, nil, fmt.Errorf("pkgname: failed to do so
mething %s",err)
  }
  ...
  // Return completed values and nil error
  return v, vv, nil
}
```

The caller should always check for errors before using values. *You should favour returning an error over returning nothing or simply a value*, even if you don't think initially you might encounter many errors, unless your function is just a few lines with no external calls. Functions rarely become simpler over time and it's always better to explicitly report errors rather than silently return zero data.

Always handle Errors

You should never discard errors using _ variables in production code. If a function returns an error, make sure you check it before using any values returned by that function. Usually if there is an error returned, values are undefined.

Either log *or* return an error

If you're logging an error, you've decided it's not important enough to handle. If you're returning an error (usually with annotation), you want the caller to handle it (which might include logging or reporting it to the user). Handle the error by logging / reporting, or return it, never both.

Don't both log and return errors:

```
if err != nil {
    // Don't do this, either deal with or return an error
    log.Printf("pkgname: failed to log stats:%s",err)
    return err
}
```

If it's not important, log and move on, if it stops processing in this function, return the error and let the caller decide how to handle it (usually to report to user and/or log):

```
func DoSomething() error {
    // For an error you can handle in this function withou
t telling the user:
    if err != nil {
        // Not important, just log the error and continue wi
th processing
        log.Printf("pkgname: failed to log stats %s",err)
    }
    ...
    // For an important error return it (usually annotate
d) and let caller decide how to report
    if err != nil {
        return fmt.Errorf("pkgname: failed to do something
 %s",err)
    }
}
```

Dave Cheney has written a talk about handling errors in go – Don't just check errors, handle them gracefully, which covers how to handle errors gracefully and avoid falling into the pitfalls outlined above.

Stack traces on errors

If you want to get a stack trace at the point of error which is
not a panic, you can use the runtime package to determine
the caller. You can also use the unofficial go-errors package,
adds stacktrace support to errors, to record the stack trace
and understand the state of execution when an error
occurred.

Finally, if you don't mind dumping a stack trace to stderr and
terminating the program, you can panic. This is useful for
debugging but less so in production programs.

Interpreting a panic stack trace

If you don't have much experience with stack traces, the
output of a panic may seem inscrutable at first. To generate a
stack trace, consider this simple program:

```go
package main

type T struct {
    s string
}

func foo(t *T) *T {
    defer panic("panic in foo")
    return t
}

func main() {
    foo(&T{})
}
```

Which produces the following panic:

```
panic: panic in foo

goroutine 1 [running]:
main.foo(0x1042bfa4, 0x0, 0x10410008, 0x0)
    /tmp/sandbox611247315/main.go:13 +0xdb
main.main()
    /tmp/sandbox611247315/main.go:18 +0x40
```

The first line gives the message passed to panic, which should be as informative as possible.

The lines after detail the crashing go routine (by default this is restricted to just the crashing one since Go 1.6). First we encounter the rather inscrutable message:

main.foo(0x1042bfa4, 0x0, 0x10410008, 0x0)

This details the function with the panic, and may provide some clues if you have a nil pointer exception as to which pointer is nil - it includes the arguments to the function (including the method struct if any, which is always the first argument), and the return values. In this case, because the program uses defer to panic, the return values are filled in before panic, hence the argument and return pointers are the same value of 0x10410008. Without the defer the second two words would both be nil.

Then the more important line which tells us which file and line the problem occurred at:

/tmp/sandbox611247315/main.go:13 +0xdb

If nothing else, this is the line you need to read, as it clearly states exactly where the problem occurred. Where you have deliberately panicked using panic() this will normally be obvious anyway, but where you have a nil pointer or index out of range it can be useful for tracking down the bug.

Remember that methods can be called on nil pointers, which can lead to subtle bugs if the callee never expects this and then tries to use the pointer as if it is initialised.

If you're debugging complex stack traces featuring many goroutines with similar stack traces you may find the panicparse library useful.

Recovering from a panic

You should recover within a **deferred function** to recover from a panic. Without a defer to make sure the recover executes last, recover will return nil and have no other effect. For example this will not work:

```
func p() {
    // Recover does nothing outwith a defer
    if r := recover(); r != nil {
        fmt.Println("recover", r)
    }
    // Something is wrong,
    // this panic will end the program
    panic("panic")
}
```

You need to use defer to recover:

```go
func main() {
    // Print calling p
    fmt.Println("calling p")
    // Call p to panic and recover
    p()
    // Recovered, print panic over
    fmt.Println("panic over")
}

func p() {
    // Defer recover to the end of this function
    defer func() {
        // Recover from panic
        if r := recover(); r != nil {
            // Print recover
            fmt.Println("recover", r)
        }
    }()

    // Something is wrong, panic
    panic("panic")
}
```

Recover must be in the same goroutine

You can only recover from panics in the current goroutine. If you have panics two goroutines deep, recovering at the top level won't catch them. For example in a web server handler which spawns a goroutine, you should protect against panics.

```go
func a() {
    panic("panic a") // this panic will crash the program
}

func main() {
    // This recover does nothing
    defer func() {
        if x := recover(); x != nil {
            fmt.Println("catch panic main")
        }
    }()
    fmt.Println("start")
    go a() // use of go means recover above won't work
    time.Sleep(1 * time.Second)
}
```

In order to catch the panic in a, a recover within that goroutine is required. Note this is not to do with function scope (removing the go before a() would allow the recover in main to work. For more detail see Handling Panics in the Go spec.

```go
func a() {
    // This recover is required to catch the panic in a
    defer func() { // recovers panic in a
        if x := recover(); x != nil {
            fmt.Println("catch panic a")
        }
    }()
    panic("panic a")
}

func main() {
        // this recover does nothing
    defer func() { // does nothing
        if x := recover(); x != nil {
            fmt.Println("catch panic main")
        }
    }()
    fmt.Println("start")
    go a() // use of go makes the recover above redundant
    time.Sleep(1 * time.Second)
}
```

Error strings

Error strings may be used inside other error strings, so they should not be capitalized (unless beginning with proper nouns or acronyms) or end with punctuation. Make them composable, so that they can be logged or annotated with other messages:

```go
// Annotating an error
return fmt.Errorf("pkgname: failed to read %s: %v", filen
ame, err)

// Returning an error without comment - prefer annotating
 if possible
return err
```

By convention, errors are annotated with the package name or function involved, to make it easy to find the error. You should try to make your error strings unique so that there is no confusion over where the error may have been emitted.

Don't panic

Panic is intended as a mechanism to report exceptional errors which require the program to exit immediately, or to report programmer error which should be fixed. You don't want to see it in production, nor should you use it to try to reproduce exceptions, which were left out of the language for a reason.

In web or api servers, you may never need to use the keyword panic, and should prefer not to. Panic is fine for programming errors, or really exceptional situations (this should never happen), but try to avoid using it if you can, especially if you're writing a library. Your users will thank you.

Don't use log.Fatalf or log.Panic

For the same reasons, don't use log.Fatalf or log.Panic except in tests or short programs, because they will halt your program without cleanup and are equivalent to calling panic.

In almost all cases you should recover gracefully from errors instead of calling a function which terminates the program.

```
// Don't do this, handle the error
log.Fatalf("broken:%s",err)
```

Asserts & Exceptions

Go doesn't provide asserts or exceptions by design. There are reasons given for both decisions in the FAQ on the Go website.

Go is boring

Hopefully by now it is clear the Go language is deliberately limited and boring. If you want a stable platform on which to build exciting programs, this is a feature, not a bug. The language keeps getting a little better with every iteration (faster, fewer pauses, bugs fixed) without breaking your programs or introducing surprising new idioms.

Less, in the case of programming languages, is more.

Glossary

Channels

Unbuffered channels combine communication — the
exchange of a value — with synchronization — guaranteeing
that two calculations (goroutines) are in a known state.

Goroutines

A goroutine is a function executing concurrently with other
goroutines in the same address space. It is a lightweight
alternative to threads invoked by using the go keyword.

Interfaces

Interfaces in Go provide a way to specify the behaviour of an
object by defining a required method set. Commonly used
interfaces like io.Writer and io.Reader usually only have very
few methods.

Slices

Slices wrap arrays to give a more general, powerful, and
convenient interface to sequences of data. Except for items
with explicit dimension such as transformation matrices, most
array programming in Go is done with slices rather than
simple arrays.

Maps

Go provides a built-in map type that implements a hash table, which is a data structure offering fast lookups, adds and deletes, but no defined order.

Mutexes

Mutexes provide a locking mechanism to ensure only one goroutine is running on a critical section of code at any one time. Typically they are used to control access to state like a map between goroutines.

Colophon

Cover image of a Rhinocerous Beetle by James Marchment as part of the Insects Unlocked Project

You can purchase this book on Amazon in Kindle and Paperback editions

The author can be found on twitter @kennygrant

Printed in Great Britain
by Amazon